SARAH WINCHESTER, MY NEIGHBOR

A Memoir by Edith Daley

Edited by Jim Fitzgerald

NEW FOREST
BOOKS

Table of Contents

Editor's Preface

The Winchester Mystery House is among America's most famous — and most haunted — houses. It attracts visitors from around the world. Everyone wants to see the curious house built by Sarah Lockwood Winchester.

Did she truly believe she would die if she ever stopped building that gargantuan home in San Jose?

History — and the house itself — suggest that's true.

Currently, the Winchester house holds about 160 rooms. (The owners keep finding more rooms, hidden behind secret panels and passageways.) But, it was rumored that Mrs. Winchester ordered over 600 rooms, each built according to her plans — and those plans may have been given to her in the secret room where she meditated... or perhaps communicated with spirits.

Many of those 600 rooms were torn down as soon as they were completed.

The Winchester house included doorways that lead nowhere, or to precipitous drops. Stairs only two inches tall, that weave back and forth like a labyrinth, eventually reaching a height of scarcely three feet. Rooms with no windows. Bathrooms with screen doors, and sometimes no working plumbing.

Was this madness, or something else?

In this book, I present a series of seven articles published in the *San Jose News*, late in 1922. They were written by librarian, writer, and poet Edith Daley (1874 - 1948), one of Mrs. Winchester's neighbors.

In flowery prose, Ms. Daley describes the house as it was during Mrs. Winchester's life, and how it changed — almost immediately — upon the owner's death.

She also tells the story of a reclusive woman who alternately shunned the outside world, and donated generously to charities.

Balancing local gossip and likely facts, Ms. Daley's story is an interesting one. It tells us more about the mysterious Mrs. Winchester, and what may have driven her to build and build... and build, all the way to her death.

I have lightly edited Ms. Daley's articles so they can be better enjoyed by today's readers. As I edited, I tried to retain the poetic style, and stay true to the facts as Ms. Daley presented them. I also tried to repair typesetting mistakes in the original articles; if I missed any, I apologize.

I believe this is an important record written by a contemporary of Mrs. Winchester. It gives us fresh insights and even more mysteries to unravel.

- J. F.

Introduction

The following was the introduction to Edith Daley's series of articles, published almost immediately following the death of Sarah Winchester.

———

The life of Mrs. Sarah L. Winchester, one of the most interesting persons who ever lived in this valley, is to be told for the first time by The News.

Edith Daley has secured a wealth of material about this unique woman, who built the famous old country place on the Winchester road.

In a sympathetic, accurate manner, Edith Daley tells the story of this woman who had a room in her home with walls, carpet, and ceiling of white satin, which no one entered but herself.

She will tell of the seven Japanese servants, employed the year round to do nothing but trim the enormous hedge surrounding the Winchester place.

She will tell why no one was ever

admitted to the Winchester place and why Mrs. Winchester annually gave thousands of dollars to various philanthropies.

This serial... promises to be one of the most interesting newspaper documents published in years.

Chapter 1

There is something about locked gates set in a towering house-hiding hedge topped with a "no admittance" sign, flanked by a gold-lettered admonition to "beware of the dog," that catches the interest. It arouses one's spirit of democracy to full fledged resentment. It awakens a lively curiosity.

That combination of sensations marked my first, close-up impression of Winchester Place. Or at least all Winchester Place that could be seen by standing on the narrow cement sidewalk outside the grounds. My nose gave an inquisitive and unapologetic nose almost gave an Eskimo salutation to the cold iron of the elaborately grilled iron gate. An entrance gate, that was securely barred. A gate through which no one, unless "on business," might enter.

Must Build or Die

The sounds of tapping hammers. The

incessant buzz of an energetic saw. The pungent smell of fresh paint.

All three filtered to the newly trimmed and forbidding cypress hedge that balance Winchester Place on the east. That's where an odd little cement sidewalk runs parallel with the broad highway that now bears the name of Winchester.

Listening to the sounds of carpentry, sniffing the odor of paint, I kept reflecting on a common report: that the rich Mrs. Winchester who lives in this mysterious house with locked gates, believes that when she stops building – she will die!

Hearsay. Just gossip of the nearby towns.

But still, there are those who, passing frequently, say that the saws have never stopped buzzing or the hammers quit tapping. And that smell of fresh paint was refreshed daily, as walls and floors were painted and repainted.

In other words: at Winchester Place, building operations are always in progress. It's so constant, the work necessitates a force of carpenters and plumbers and painters hired by the year.

Hole in the Hedge

Snip, snip! I dislike the odor of fresh paint; but this enticed.

Pound, pound, tap, tap. Noise is abhorrent; but these hammers called.

Buzz, Buzz, Buzz! What in the world was it all about? More walls going up or more walls coming down in a smother of plaster and broken lathe – that the mistress of Winchester Place might live long and prosper?

Standing there, trying to get a clear view of the tree and shrubbery of skewered house, I shook the locked gates. I shook them until their fancy iron curly-cues rattled.

Pausing, I said to myself: "I'd give a dollar to walk in that garden."

Not that it promised more of blossoms or beauty than any other garden of my intimate acquaintance. Instead, that hedge and those signs triggered an outraged feeling of democracy. I believe in beauty being shared, since God made it all.

And, after mentioning that purely fictitious dollar which I really wouldn't have given to walk in that aristocratically isolated rich woman's garden, I must have inadvertently pulled a bit on the leash of my hand.

Instantly, as if he understood, my dog pulled forward against the leash. He pointed an eager nose at a ragged hole in the tall hedge. Then he whined coaxingly to be allowed to go in an adventure.

For a minute a temptation, aided and abetted by that bit of democratic resentment, tugged at my will as the dog pulled on the leash.

But he was a small dog, and tremendously dear to me. I feared that the beast we were supposed to "beware" was a huge shaggy creature of fang-tearing ferocity.

Anyway, there was probably a dire penalty for trespassing. I'm sure they'd have said so, if I met the lady of the manor or one of her henchmen, and attempted an excuse of a lost dog.

Unhappy Old House

It wouldn't do. We went right away from there. But not until I had exchanged a brief stare at the great broad-based house.

It seemed to stare back at me through a tangle of bamboo, with queerly placed windows that looked like eyes.

I even dared to smile at the old house. Who feared it anyway, even with its lofty hedges and two keep-out signs? Who feared a fussily dressed and ginger-breaded old house?

As I gazed at it, it seemed to rambled about without any particular architectural intention. In fact, it smiled rather pitifully under its faded yellow paint. It reminded me of an aging woman who rouges and powders her face in a futile effort to look young.

Poor old house. Poor big old house? Poor fat old house, trying to appear complacent. Instead, it managed only to look restless and dissatisfied and, I suppose, bored. A little gray with age.

And what of she who lived there? They said she was alone, except for the companionship of one niece. One loyal niece who served as companion, private secretary, and personal maid. Were they happy – these two?

They had money, of course. They also lived in rather splendid isolation. If reports were true, the old lady was generous, even a benefactor of many charities. But did the Winchester millions deliver enough of life for Mrs. Sarah Winchester of Winchester Place?

Would Come Back

"Queer old place," I said to the dog, tugging gently on his leash.

"Poor old place. Pretentious and sort of forlorn. New, but also very, very old.

"Doesn't look happy. Doesn't sound happy – not with this chorus of saw and hammer to which progress is trying to write the words."

Rather thoughtfully we left the iron gates, and I grimaced at the "beware of the dog" sign. With a sigh, I pulled my dear little dog away from another enticing hole in the hedge.

"Never mind, old chap," I comforted. "There are other gardens where we are welcome. This looks like a rabbit-less place anyway.

"And very likely there is no cat.

"Never mind! One of these days I'm going to walk right through that gate. Yes, I'll walk in that garden and sit on a red-painted bench in the sun. And then I'll look at that queer house right in the face!"

And with those words, we turned away from the house and continued our walk.

"Sarah Winchester is Dead"

And, without meaning a word of it, it came true for me.

It happened one day, when I went out by myself. Poor dog. He'd given up on my promises to visit the Winchester garden.

Yes, the years had passed between the morning when I looked in in the morning when I went in – through the big gates at Winchester Place.

Day by day, year by year, rumors about Winchester Place had flown thick and fast. Speculation spilled over in every neighboring town and hamlet.

More and more, one heard the strange theory that the rich woman who lived in the house behind the hedge believed that she had to keep on building in order to keep on living.

And more and more people came to believe that there must be some truth in the common report. After all, year after year, the carpenters and the plumbers and the painters remained at Winchester Place. Day and night, passers-by heard the sounds of their hammers and saws, and wrinkled their noses at the smell of the fresh paint never ceased.

With each passing day, the great house grew. It grew top-heavy and lopsided. It grew to become a monstrous crime committed in the name of architecture.

Architecturally, according to those who knew, it was neither "fish, fowl or good red herring."

The number of rooms increased, but the family still number two. Just Mrs. Winchester and her niece, if stories were true.

But of course few could confirm that, for the "no admittance" and "beware of the dog" signs were forbidding. Mrs. Winchester - and perhaps her niece - defended their privacy almost as ferociously as the pack of snarling and vicious dogs were rumored to patrol the grounds.

Guest room after guest room was added; but there were no guests.

Years passed as, inevitably, years do.

And then, one morning not long ago, each of us picked up the morning paper.

We read: "Sarah Winchester is summoned by death."

A heart stopped beating.

The uplifted hammers paused – and never struck.

The buzzing saws fell to silence – a silence that dropped like a pall over the Winchester Place.

Neither building nor tearing down could stay the touch of age and illness and death.

Chapter 2

After death visited Winchester Place, one of the long-locked iron gates was left open.

And through that gate, on a sunny September morning, I walked down a gray gravel driveway.

It led into the garden that I had once said jokingly, "I would give a dollar to enter."

The garden seemed entirely unconscious that death had passed that way. The flowers bloomed as yesterday, the tall trees whispered together; but she who love them was not there to hear.

No pounding hammer, no rasping saw. The insistent smell of fresh paint had drifted into nothingness.

In the garden, I felt only the warmth of autumn sunshine and savored the faint breath of late roses.

An aged Chinaman, probably one of Mrs. Winchester's legendary gardeners, went about his affairs as if he were alone in that September world.

A complacent black-and-white cat sat with its tail primly drawn around its feet, and purred with content.

The ancient gardener and the satisfied cat did not care who came – or went.

Beautiful trees, touched with autumn, flecked the gray path with shadows. They softly scattered upon it the leaves that were weary of summer – as Sarah Winchester, age 82, had been worn with life.

The once primly kept hedge grew raggedly at the top – but happily, as if its cypress branches reached gladly out to the sun, and rejoiced in the newfound freedom.

Innumerable birds twittered and fluttered in the treetops. Nearby, a row of towering palm trees marched along the roadway inside the south entrance to Winchester Place. Their great trunks seemed soft in the afternoon light, near an emerald ribbon of blossoming rose bushes.

Around a fountain just inside the gates, sleepy looking stone frogs seemed to be waiting for something. Perhaps they longed for the living urge of water that had ceased to fall in the wide cement basin.

One clump of weeds intruded in the

fountain. Just one clump of venturesome weeds and a few crisply rustling brown-gold leaves that still held enough of life to stir at the whim of the wind.

Farther down the drive – still inside the wire enclosure – a sculptured deer held its unchanging pose on a rock pedestal overgrown with ivy.

And beyond the ivy-covered pedestal with its suggestion of the freedom of great forests, the garden of Winchester Place stretched toward the huge house and spread around it. Perhaps it hoped to lend a perfection to the architecture that, even now, has a sad lack of beauty.

If architecture is "frozen music," then this house is a clash of discords! But, big, awkward, and overgrown, it takes the garden homage offered at its wide-spreading foundations. Perhaps it gained something of dignity from the poise of perfect trees and fragrant flowers.

I tried to see the gargantuan house more kindly. Poor old house. It was not its fault that its mistress acted upon every architectural whim, alternately building and tearing down, and then building again.

Cypress and Palm sentinels

The yellow-painted house seemed far-flung, like Kipling's battle line in *Recessional*, "God of our fathers, known of old, / Lord of our far-flung battle line, Beneath whose awful hand we hold / Dominion over palm and pine — Lord God of Hosts, be with us yet, / Lest we forget — lest we forget!"

Was it dominion that Mrs. Winchester held, or did it have a hold over her? We may never know.

As I gazed at the house, I saw that the paint had weathered to a soft deep creaminess.

Now the wide drive circles a plot of velvet lawn, lifting to flowering clumps of pinky lavender hydrangeas. In turn, they look up to cypresses and palms, one of each standing guard on either side.

Between the guarding trees rise is a wall of feathery bamboo which effectually hides the house from the highway. I see garden seats here and there, in sun or shadow as one desires. And I, remembering, chose the red-painted one in the sun.

Sitting there – deserted by even the complacent cat — I forgot the glory of the day. I was almost overcome by a feeling of sorrow that the woman who caused all this beauty would never walk here again.

And, thinking of her, of the Sarah Winchester about whom there is been so much of conjecture and speculation, my feelings soften. Was her only sin that she dared to be different? That she chose to live her life in her own way?

I turned to face the venerable house that, touched with the light of sympathy, seemed pathetic rather than architecturally absurd.

House Never Finished

Such a surprising house! Finished – and unfinished! More than 40 years in building – and not built yet! Even at the front of the house, weatherbeaten boards testified that further building operations had been thought and planned – and passed on.

Commonly Discussed Subject

A maze of gray-painted buildings behind the great house tempted me to investigate further.

Not far from the kitchens, lay a small pile of new lumber. But for what purpose was it to be used – who can tell now? Porch or pergola, wide windows or narrow door, guest room or corridor to nowhere? And what does it matter – now?

It serves only to recall the commonly discussed subject of Mrs. Winchester's belief that if she stopped building, she would die.

Those who know say that the building operations never did stop at Winchester place. In fact, it was never finished.

Room after room was added. Wall after wall fell that rooms might be enlarged or rebuilt, according to a newer plan.

Never for a working day during Mrs. Winchester's years of occupancy were building operations suspended – not until death came with its strange deep hush.

Into the Deep Silence

A long, many-windowed, covered passageway led out from the south end of the big house. It connected with a great conservatory filled with luxuriantly growing ferns, palms and flowering begonias.

Beyond that glass-roofed place of living beauty, other underground hot houses were built close to the extensive propagation beds.

And just west of the conservatory, I could glimpse a full-grown colony of buildings. I knew they included servants quarters, the palatial stables of other days, plus one old-fashioned structure modernized for use as a garage.

Nearby, one wonderful wisteria vine covers a vast expanse of gray wall. Flowers in profusion are everywhere. They flourish everywhere in purple and pink, as well as the lavender and white of asters.

Row after row of chrysanthemums promise late blooms of feathery gold and white and mauve and rich red. All of these blossoms were planned by the quiet-loving woman who planned everything at Winchester Place – and who has gone away into a silence that makes her restful garden seemed a place of sharp sound.

Chapter 3

Something about the rambling, oddly constructed house at Winchester Place — something strange and rather pathetic — set me to wondering about the woman who had lived there for over 40 years.

She was a recluse, in a sense of the word unusual in our stirring modern times.

No social life.

No children.

Few relatives.

Whatever lightness and joy entered her isolated life, seemed to have done so by way of her constant planning and building and never-ceasing rebuilding of this overgrown house. If it could speak, surely it would tell something interesting.

What of Mrs. Winchester's eccentricities? Reports listed many.

She was said never to leave her carriage or her automobile to enter a shop in town. She waited quietly while her personal representative made purchases of necessary clothing and household linens.

What lay in back of it all? What could

have the power to send a woman of refinement and great wealth into a life so far apart from the world?

Acquainted with Grief

Sorrow she had suffered. It was the heartbreaking sorrow that scars the very soul of a loving woman.

Her husband died – some say of the dreaded white plague – and, as she buried him, she also stood beside the grave of her only child.

There is no way of measuring the havoc wrought by grief for loved ones in the tender heart of a woman. None may say what lay hidden by the efforts to adjust life to immeasurable loss.

Remembering Mrs. Winchester, perhaps those of us who little understood, called them "eccentricities."

We all have them. But Mrs. Winchester's wealth and prominence caused her to be rather pitilessly watched by eyes eager to see something unusual.

Few who knew her well were willing to talk about the life of the lady of

Winchester Place.

But from one who, for a period of 10 years was a visitor at the great yellow house behind the tall cypress hedges, I have much interesting information. Each detail was kindly given.

Through his eyes, I saw Sarah Winchester as a woman with a grieving mother-heart. I understood the sorrow of one whose years of lonely widowhood were marked by more than ordinarily generous giving. And giving is what she did, year after year, to all charitable institutions considered worthy. Beautiful giving – because it sought no publicity.

But, even seeing her sympathetically, a mystery remains. As I look at some of the more exceptional aspects of Winchester Place and its owner's life, I find no reasonable, earthly explanations.

Built Seven-Story Tower

About 40 years ago — according to my informant — and following the death of her husband, Mrs. Winchester came to make her home here.

She purchased the property now known as Winchester Place, a tract containing about 50 acres. Moving at once into the comparatively small house on the place, she instituted her never-ending building operations. One of her first acts was to set out the cypress hedge which is now a landmark.

The small house grew to a residence of 38 rooms. Over the years that followed, those rooms increased until Winchester Place became a great mansion of 102 rooms, some of which were destroyed by the earthquake.

In the center of the great house, there lifted a seven-story tower in which a hydraulic elevator was installed. Later, that tower, shaken down by the earthquake, was not rebuilt.

White Satin Room

The most unusual realm, according to the one who frequently visited the house, was the room at the base of the tower.

No one ever entered into this room except Mrs. Winchester.

It was floored with white. The walls and seats were white – spotless white satin. There was only one window, closely-curtained.

Across this drawn curtain a woman's shadow sometimes passed. The eerie shadow was all that curious eyes were ever able to see of what took place in this strange room to which Mrs. Winchester is said to have frequently repaired.

Motifs Like Targets

The first decorative motifs on the house are said to have been — strangely — like painted targets. To even the most casual observer, they're clearly suggestive of the great industry — the Winchester Repeating Rifles — from which Mrs. Winchester derived her enormous income.

Cupolas appealed to her. In fact, it was not long before the roofs fairly blossomed with cupolas.

Walking in the garden, if she chanced to look up toward an apparently lonely cupola, Mrs. Winchester would call her head carpenter.

She'd point to the object of her attention and then to an empty corner of the roof and say, "Put another cupola over there!"

In the days before the earthquake, the flock of cupolas, big and little, numbered 15.

For years, so says my informant, Winchester Place kept a staff of between 18 and 22 carpenters, plumbers, and painters.

These workmen were employed by the year. They were required to do excellent work, and no lumber less than perfect was permitted to go into the building of the great house, with its accompanying colony of assorted structures.

Upon one occasion Mrs. Winchester ordered a large amount of "clear lumber."

When the lumber was delivered, she walked to where it was piled, took one look at it and said, "Take it away!"

She had seen two or three knots, and no imperfect lumber should go into the making of her home. Every bit of construction was supposed to be permanent and the workmanship as perfect as was humanly possible.

But apparently, perfection meant little.

The most solidly built walls were torn out. Perfectly laid floors were ripped up. The smoothest plaster fell in a dusty shower – that Winchester Place might never cease to echo with the sounds of progress, which, in this place, meant building.

Beautiful "Prism Hall"

The house has an entrance hall that might grace a palace. It is called "Prism Hall," but few — if any — are said to have entered by the wide doors that lead into this marvelous place.

In fact, the doors were kept securely locked.

This hall, about 8x40 feet in size, has wainscoting of prisms solidly set so that no wood is visible.

There are thousands of these prisms so that one walking the length of the hall is multiplied by the countless rainbow reflections.

"What is the ceiling decoration in Prism Hall?" I inquired.

My companion, who'd walked there, smiled and shook his head. "I don't know. The effect of the prisms is so overwhelming that one never thinks to glance at the ceiling.

"Three men were imported from Chicago to set the prisms which cost many thousands of dollars.

"The hall contains no furniture except some solid mahogany pedestals holding rear Italian marbles – the Venus de Milo, Winged Victory, and Bacchus, among others."

Little Reception Room

All who came to Winchester Place — as well as the secretary, servants, head carpenter, and gardener — were said to always enter by a side staircase. They were received by Mrs. Winchester in a small room near the head of the stairs, a room very plainly furnished and without a single hint of luxury.

In this plain little room, she is said to have received her nephew upon the occasion of his only visit to her.

The story of this visit shows the remarkable brevity of her communication even with a member of her family.

Apparently, this nephew, named Sprague — a Shakespearean actor — once telegraphed from New York to Mrs. Winchester.

The message stated that his physician had ordered him to Carlsbad for his health.

"If you do not send me $5000, I will die," Sprague said in his wire.

Mrs. Winchester did not reply.

Sometime later, that very much alive nephew appeared at the Garden Theater in San Jose.

After the play, he dressed immaculately and went to call at Winchester Place.

He rang the bell — and got in. But he was not admitted by way of the front entrance and Prism Hall.

Instead, he had to use the side staircase, and he was received by his aunt in the little room at the head of the stairs.

It should be noted that Mrs. Winchester never received visitors unless her secretary was present.

On this occasion, as soon as Sprague entered — even before any exchange of greetings — Mrs. Winchester turned to her secretary and said, "Bring me my checkbook!"

When the checkbook was presented to her, she turned to her nephew and said, "So you are not dead."

"No, I am not dead," he replied. "I am a Shakespearean actor, and you are one of the wealthiest women in the United States.

"I need money. If you will give me $50,000 now you may eliminate me from your will."

According to my informant, Mrs. Winchester silently wrote a check for $50,000, handed it to her nephew, waved him away, and the family incident was closed.

Chapter 4

There is a possibility that fear of bodily harm may have had something to do with the isolation of Mrs. Winchester's life.

Many among the extremely wealthy have suffered from this kind of fear. Often, it's brought to sharp intensity by an unexpected incident.

In the old days, in the rear of the great house, there was a wine cellar stocked with tier after tier of the rarest vintages.

It is related that one morning, as she inspected different parts of her property, Mrs. Winchester visited this wine cellar.

Once inside the door she stood absolutely still and gasped.

On the clean surface of a furnace pipe there was the imprint of a black hand!

Sarah fled and immediately gave orders for the wine cellar to be double locked.

"And to this day," said my informant, "it is quite likely that the double locks are still there.

"Mrs. Winchester said that she felt

sure a bomb had been placed there, and the house would be blown up."

On another occasion she evidenced the same fear of destruction.

During the Spanish-American war it happened that a Mexican was among the men employed on the place. When his work was done the foreman asked that the man be paid and discharged as his services were no longer required.

But Mrs. Winchester demurred. She said that, while the war was on, it would not do to discharge the Mexican. He might be angry and blow up the place. For more than a year she paid him wages though he did no work.

Theory of Fear

My informant has a theory about Mrs. Winchester's overwhelming fear. This theory theory has a foundation in things that Mrs. Winchester said within his hearing.

On many occasions, she was heard to say, in so many words, that because her income that came from rifles, and ammunition that take life, she felt that she must give much to humanity.

Somewhere in this recognition of the deadliness of the product of that industry — the one that that gave her income — lay the reason for her recurring fear.

So, she did give to others, and with a generosity that seemed to know no bounds.

She never, or rarely, gave to individuals. Instead, she donated to accredited institutions, especially to the New Haven tuberculosis hospital. Those thousands of dollars have given hope and health to thousands of patients who were waiting hopelessly for death.

My informant shared many other stories of Mrs. Winchester's sometimes-impulsive generosity.

Once, while out driving, Mrs. Winchester and a companion passed the Women's Relief Corps Home at Evergreen.

Mrs. Winchester inquired about the institution. As soon as she learned its purpose, she sent her secretary to ask if any financial help was needed.

And then, without leaving the carriage, she wrote a check for a large amount, and sent it in with the usual request that there be absolutely no publicity.

This incident in the life of the woman we called strange, because she chose to live by a different plan, was repeated many times.

There is no way to measure the good she did with her on ostentatious — and often anonymous — gifts that continued through all the long years.

Read All Newspapers

Mrs. Winchester detested publicity as far as she was personally concerned. However, she subscribed to all the newspapers and many good magazines, and read them all.

She owned a magnificent library and read deeply, being especially fond of Shakespeare.

Sarah was intensely interested in religious cults and "isms," as well. She delved into Christian Science, Spiritualism, and East Indian philosophy.

Her library contained all of H. Rider Haggard's works, and she is said to have read "She" many times, until the book was battered and worn.

Knitting was her most feminine diversion, and she was often seen with a bit of knitting, her adept fingers making the needles fly.

The great place boasted its own gas plant, with gas furnishing both light and heat.

Every fireplace held a gas log; there were no blazing wood fires. And all the lights were subdued, no flare of light being permitted at Winchester Place.

Amusing Incident of Visit

Visitors were never permitted to meet with Mrs. Winchester – not even admitted to the house — when they were bold enough to ring the bell.

To nearly everyone, Mrs. Winchester was never "at home."

She neither sought nor denied company other than the companionship of her private secretary and the association of her own veiled thoughts.

This was widely known and respected.

Once in a while, someone called – only to be turned away. No matter how kindly the spirit of their visit, each met the same rebuff.

One amusing incident is told of a call at Winchester Place. According to the story, Charles M. Shortridge – then editor of a local paper – donned his best clothes and put on the glory of a silk hat. Then, he took it upon himself to pay his social respects to Mrs. Winchester.

She Was Not at Home

Nothing daunted the redoubtable Charles. He smoothed his silk hat and put it away. And, after thinking about what Sarah's rebuff, he came up with a plan.

The next social column in his newspaper reported some astonishing information. It said, "Charles M. Shortridge was recently entertained by Mrs. S. L. Winchester."

Considering the lady's dislike of publicity, perhaps that society notice was sufficient revenge for a locked door!

Held Prisoner in Hothouse

My informant had stored up many memories of Winchester Place. The next deals with an amusing episode and Sarah's continued refusal to see visitors.

At one time, *The Examiner* — a paper from San Francisco — sent some cameramen to Winchester Place.

"There used to be lookouts stationed in the grounds," my informant explained. "On this occasion, word was taken to Mrs. Winchester as soon as the invaders near the gates.

"It happened that she was paying a morning visit to the hothouses.

"Not having time to reach the house, she fled into the underground depths of her conservatories. This one was only partially underground, and heated to the right temperature for plants — but a trifle overheated for a human being.

"The cameramen refused to be denied access to the legendary Mrs. Winchester. They stayed, and took their time setting up a few pictures.

"When they finally went away a

servant tapped on the glass roof of the conservatory. Mrs. Winchester, more dead than alive, managed to escape from her self-chosen prison.

"Apparently, she liked discomfort better than she did callers – but this time the discomfort was almost too much for her."

Tea Room Without Tea

The main living room Winchester Place was paneled in solid mahogany, furnished with rare old Sheratons, and given a note of beauty by Antwerp blue hangings. The oak floor is covered deep with rare Oriental rugs.

It is said to be an exquisite apartment.

It is in this room that not one but *two* safes hold the valuable gold plate that is used every day upon the table in the soft-lighted dining room.

Between the main living room and the music room — which occupies the extreme south end of the house, downstairs — there are a number of interesting realms.

One of them is a Japanese room in

which the furnishings, rugs, screens, tapestries, pictures, and bits of rare pottery are all imported from Japan.

Next to the Japanese room is the tea room – in which tea is never served.

It is exquisitely appointed, and has been kept so for years, but there are no guests.

In fact, there have never been any guests to partake of this kind of gracious hospitality.

Mrs. Winchester always had her tea served wherever she chanced to be. Often, that was in the little unpretentious room upstairs where she transacted her manifold business affairs. At other times, it was out on the terrace if she happened to feel the lure of her beautiful garden.

It does not require much imagination to picture that wonderfully appointed tea room – empty. And, at the same time, a lonely gray-haired woman taking her tea in solitary state.

I like to think of her, relaxing in a far corner of an isolated veranda, or out on the terrace – a happier place – companioned by her own deep thoughts.

Chapter 5

Rich mahogany panels and antique gold velour draperies added elegance to the dining room at Winchester Place.

It was in that beautiful room, night after night, that a trim maid served dinner.

The woman who was an epicure as well as a recluse, sat — often, alone — at the table.

Near her, soft lights in solid gold candelabra brought out the exquisiteness of rare gold plate upon which the solitary but sumptuous meal was served.

No butler at this cypress-hedged house – never!

Chinese in the big kitchen. Japanese in the gardens.

But for personal service, quiet efficient maids. One of them did nothing except see to it that the bowls and vases of the big house were constantly filled with fresh flowers from the gardens and extensive conservatories.

The largest conservatories were on the second floor, not adjacent to other rooms.

In other words, one can't restful glimpses of palm and fern and blossoming plants. At least not across a vista of Oriental rugs, priceless tapestries, and rare old furniture.

The finest conservatories, so it is said, were set apart. They did not share close companionship with rooms intimate to the life of the lonely recluse.

My informant could not explain this, and — to this day — it seems particularly odd. Oh, how I would love to ask Mrs. Winchester questions about her home!

Safes for Gold Plate

There is a story about Winchester Place, related to six safes Sarah installed to hold valuables.

The largest safe — with a smaller one on top — was in the living room. Every night, after the gold service has been used and the lights put out in the golden candelabra, a servant began his procession from the dining room to the big safe in the living room.

One can easily picture the stately old lady who bore a striking resemblance to

Queen Victoria. I can almost see her sitting in a lonely state before a table spread with solid gold plate. I imagine her epicurean pleasure in the triumphs of her excellent chef.

I hope it was enough to fill the emptiness of her everyday life, so far removed from ordinary, friendly human beings.

And later, the last course served, the last candle snuffed, the servant would gather up in his arm the loads of valuable plate. Thus he'd begin his nightly pilgrimage to the place of safekeeping, in the big living room.

Wonderful Music Room

Mrs. Winchester, always fond of music, is said to have played the piano — but not with any degree of skill. Her delight in the "concord of sweet sounds" impelled her to add a music room in the house.

This room, occupying the extreme south end of the lower floor, has walls and a ceiling of stucco work. It was beautifully frescoed by a famous mural painter brought to Winchester Place especially for this task.

In one end of the great room Mrs. Winchester installed the finest "Orchestrall" that money could buy. There was a magnificent grand piano here, and several other equally good instruments in other parts of the house.

A pianola, a phonograph – and every one of its followers showing improvement – occupied places in the wonderful room. Mrs. Winchester's collection even included a rare violin — which no one ever played. That instrument sat alone, listening to the music in a state of seclusion greater than that of the woman who bought it and placed it here – in its eternal silence.

Tried to Hire Bostonians

Mrs. Winchester's love of music was so deep that, at one time, only a train schedule prevented the great house from being made gloriously happy by beautiful music.

On this occasion, The Bostonians came

to San Jose.   Mrs. Winchester's private secretary attended the theater that night and came home with eyes shining and voice growing with the charm of the music.

Mrs. Winchester, with the impulsive directness that seemed a character contradiction, gave orders that the manager of the Bostonians should be found – by telephone.

When he paused in his preparations of packing to catch a late train and hurry away to another engagement, he was advised of the caller. Then his astonishment knew no bounds when heard the question that came over the wire.

"What will you charge to come to Winchester place and repeat this evening's performance?"

Covering his surprise, the manager asked "Is there a theater?"

"No," answered the strange voice.

"Will there be an audience?" The man must've thought the caller a bit mad.

"Only two," was the calm reply, followed by a repetition of the request for the performance – that night!

The manager explained that he could

not possibly put aside his prearranged schedule to accommodate this persistent woman. As she persisted, the manager gathered the idea that cost meant nothing – as indeed, it didn't. Nevertheless, he could not accommodate her request. No amount of money would change that.

By chance, my informant had been the little secretary's escort on that night. So, he was privy to the unusual, late night call. He says that $20,000 would not have caused Mrs. Winchester to think twice.

When she greatly desired a thing — as she longed for this concert in her Winchester Place music room — no amount of money seemed too much to pay for the satisfaction – of a whim.

Express Loads of Vases

Mrs. Winchester's income was so large that she had difficulty in knowing what to do with it, even after the enormous checks were given to charities.

For example, one day she and her secretary were driving through the streets of San Jose. They sat comfortably in the

Victoria which was familiar to everyone.

Mrs. Winchester was said never to have left her conveyance – the Victoria or limousine – to enter a shop. Her secretary was her personal representative on all occasions.

This day, passing along San Jose's Second Street, Mrs. Winchester's attention was caught by some rare Chinese vases. They were displayed in the window of the "City of Peking," a miniature "Sing Fat" store. A man named Yan Tai was the proprietor. The bit of beauty that caught Sarah's fancy was a goddess figure. It was made of rare apple onyx.

The secretary went into the store and returned with the smiling Chinese proprietor.

Mrs. Winchester — in her choicest pidgin English — asked the price of the vase.

"$900," was laconic answer.

Mrs. Winchester asked other clearly worded sentences, hoping to be understood by the Chinaman. Gradually, she learned that there were many more valuable vases in the little shop.

Her eyes lit up with pleasure, and she signified that she wanted the man to bring all that he had to her home.

Nodding his head, the still smiling Chinese bowed himself away

"Call him back," said the interested rich woman. "He didn't ask my name or where to bring the vases."

Into the shop went the patient secretary.

Again the urbane Oriental came out – still smiling.

And then, to Mrs. Winchester's evident chagrin, he addressed her in the most beautiful English. "You are Mrs. Winchester," he said. "I will bring my valuable vases to your home tomorrow morning."

Beauty Has Been Served

True to his word, Yan Tai appeared at Winchester Place the next morning, accompanied by a Chinese assistant and two express wagon loads of vases.

Then the unusual happened: He and his assistant were bidden to enter.

Inside one of the big rooms, Mrs. Winchester, Yan Tai, and the Chinese assistant sat down on the floor, Oriental fashion.

One after another the beautiful wares were displayed. One after another were set aside as purchases for Winchester Place.

Before the end of the exhibition, the rare apple onyx piece was accompanied by most of the other expensive items from the express wagons.

Yan Tai and his Chinese assistant went away.

The express wagons were empty – and Yan Tai's bank account much fuller. The beautiful things made in the faraway Orient remained, to live in quiet seclusion, even unto this day.

And who is to say that beauty has not been served? The vases have known no sordid mess. Most have been left unsullied and untouched. Others have gladly given themselves to the task of holding the rarest blossoms from the great conservatories of Winchester Place.

All have served the purpose for which they were created, and — no doubt —

brought great joy to Mrs. Winchester.

Chapter 6

Mrs. Sarah Winchester was fond of dogs and horses. She owned three splendidly matched teams — sorrel, bay and black — and took great pride in them. In the days of the Victoria, no ordinary harness would do as full dress for these beautiful teams.

So, she purchased a solid gold, mounted harness.

Her coachman wore livery with buttons of solid silver, bearing the initials "S.L.W." In San Jose, in his formal immobility, he was a familiar sight to both the grown-ups and the children. Particularly to the children.

When one of her superb teams pranced into town and was drawn up with a flourish in front of a shop, Mrs. Winchester's coachman, rather than the interesting lady herself, became the center of attraction for juvenile eyes.

Sometimes, his wait at the curb was prolonged. But never once, no matter how sorely he might be tempted, did the coachman's eyes turn to the right or left.

He was unquestionably a human being – but trained as his strange employer like her retainers to be trained, in absolute obedience. His demeanor — and perhaps his role — was furniture-like inanimateness. The only exception was when he was handling the ribbons over the backs of the beautiful horses. They were his pride, as they were hers.

They say that to this day, the Victoria, the gold-mounted harness, and the livery with the silver buttons are all kept at Winchester Place.

Eventually, the horses gave place to the two fine Renault cars, and a number of other automobiles.

And now, the sunset days of the three matched teams are being spent in green pastures on Mrs. Winchester's Atherton estate.

Vacation at Del Monte

At one time, so the story goes, Mrs. Winchester unexpectedly announced that she and her secretary would spend a gala week at Del Monte.

The secretary was to dress the part of a wealthy seaside visitor. So, in San Francisco, seven rarely exquisite gowns were purchased, one for each evening of the week.

At the appointed time, the Victoria rolled up to the door. The lady of Winchester Place and her little secretary entered, and were driven rapidly in the direction of their chosen hostelry.

Sumptuous apartments were waiting.

The sun shone golden, and the blue bay danced a welcome. Maybe the heart of the patient little secretary missed a beat or two in expectation of the unusual experience of a really good time. But it was a vacation as weird as daily life at the great yellow house behind the cypress hedge.

Each evening at the Del Monte, the secretary appeared in the brilliantly lighted dining room where all eyes feasted upon the expansiveness and beauty of her different down. But she always dined alone.

Yes, Mrs. Winchester had all her meals served in the privacy of her apartment. After a week of that sort of polarity, the horses were arrayed in their gold mounted harness and the Victoria rolled home again.

And so the great vacation ended.

Bought Peace and Quiet

One privilege was Mrs. Winchester's by reason of her enormous wealth. It is something which does not bear a very deep stamp of eccentricity. Many of lesser means wish they were able to do the same thing.

If the grand lady disliked whatever happened to be next door or across the road, she purchased it – and removed the objectionable.

For example, shortly after coming into possession of her Atherton property, a prominent house on millionaires Row, she went there. Her plan was to remain there for some weeks.

However, her first evening in her wonderful new home was greatly disturbed.

Apparently, her neighbors — who are

also owners of a palatial residence — were jolly souls. They enjoyed company.

That is why Mrs. Winchester's first evening of prepared solitude did not go as planned.

The neighbors had steady outbursts of merriment, dancing, light laughter, and — perhaps worst of all — *jazz music.*

Early the following morning, Mrs. Winchester sent an emissary to find out if the next-door property could be bought, and at what price.

She immediately purchased it and never entered or rented it.

Likewise, when the Corbett estate in Burlingame passed into her ownership, it included a houseboat costing several thousands of dollars. But then she never boarded it!

Loved that Spanish Piece

There was much evidence of her love of music. One could see it in the fine and exquisite musical instruments she owned, and some that she played.

The following event occurred during

the years when one or two young men were permitted to enter Winchester Place, to pay their ardent court to the secretary.

According to the stories, there were summer evenings when the young folks sat under the big trees of Winchester Place – visiting, singing, or watching the silver stars. Those evenings were gay with the music of mandolin and guitar.

With the first twang of strings, with the first broken chord, Mrs. Winchester's upstairs window would be softly opened. She would listen and enjoy it all silently.

But then, when the last haunting strain of a particular Spanish melody failed, she leaned out from her casement – quite like a lady of old Spain – and entreated them to "please play it again!"

One night, the open-air conversation turned to the stars. One of the young men, a bit of an astronomer, had lately spent an entire night at the Earth end of the big telescope at Lick Observatory.

As he spoke, not far from Mrs. Winchester's open window, he related how he watched "little moon after little moon come up."

He talked about the apparent canals on the planet Mars, explaining that many scientists hold to the belief that Mars is inhabited.

Then, he described the remarkable telescope with its 36 inch lens and the cost of $1 million.

That's when there was evidence of intense interest from the darkened window upstairs.

Mrs. Winchester, who had been listening, immediately wanted to know what it would cost to build a bigger observatory with a larger telescope than the one at Lick Observatory.

It was a project she wanted to pursue in the future, and took very seriously.

Sale with a Joker

Mrs. Winchester kept her own counsel. But an idea — an interesting, exciting idea — had entered her mind. It lingered for several months after she overheard the astronomical conversation on the lawn.

After that, Sarah's exceptionally heavy

mail became even heavier, by reason of the many communications from astronomers and builders of telescopes.

It became clear that she entertained a tentative plan of building a great observatory on the property across from her Winchester Place home.

And that brings to mind the story of how that property came into her possession. This is a true story of a real estate deal with a joker in it.

Just across the road from Winchester Place, on the east, sat a tract of level land. It was as level as a floor and carpeted with wildflowers. And it seemed to be fairly crying to high heaven – and the wide awake real estate agent – to be sold to somebody.

One bright young chap decided that "somebody" should be Mrs. Winchester.

The tract lay adjacent to her property, she could afford to purchase, and if he had any selling ability, he was sure the deal was going through.

He and another young man put their heads together and evolved a beautiful scheme, beautiful in its simplicity.

Shortly after that scheme had its

inception, one of the two real estate agents chanced to be in conversation with a member of Mrs. Winchester's household.

"Do you know," said the astute young man, "that there is a rumor to the effect that a roadhouse is going to be built on the property across the street from Winchester Place? "

Checkbook in Action

The member of Mrs. Winchester's staff recoiled in horror. "A roadhouse! How awful! Just wait until Mrs. Winchester hears it," was the reply.

When the great lady heard it, she did the expected thing. Her checkbook came into action, double-quick marching time.

She bought that tract of land and it was there she planned to build her observatory — the one which should house a telescope larger than the one at Mount Hamilton.

One of her friends believed that Sarah's idea had something to do with her unknown religious belief. The beliefs that, many nights, brought her to the white satin room.

In his opinion, she believed in life on the other planets, perhaps as the beautiful abode of departed spirits.

With an immense telescope, she may have reason, there would be a possibility of seeing these other human habitations where her loved and lost awaited her coming.

Of course, that is speculation. Idle speculation.

No one knew positively of Mrs. Winchester's religious beliefs. "She was supposed to be a Spiritualist," says someone who knew her, "but there was never any proof of it."

Chapter 7 - Conclusion

Mrs. Winchester was known to dislike lawyers and doctors, although one prominent attorney became her friend and advisor.

Of course, due to the size of the estate, Sarah's will occupied considerable time. She wrote it and rewrote it, adding many codicils.

But she did not consult an attorney as she wrote. Each time she'd change the document to her immediate satisfaction, it went, by messenger, to a lawyer in town.

Then the telephone calls began. They started with the matter of whether or not things were according to the literary and legal rules for the last wills and testaments.

It was a necessary part of Mrs. Winchester's life.

Likewise, while disliking doctors, the lady of the great house employed a nurse by the year. That became necessary when, after age 70 or so, the infirmities of the flesh kept her more closely confined, and in self-chosen isolation.

But even then, despite her pain and age, she was alert to every building demand in her "progression or death" program.

For example, though Sarah depended upon a wheelchair as a means of locomotion, her visits to the white satin room continued, though she was accompanied by a nurse. However, the nurse could go only as far as the door.

Beyond that portal, none might enter except the woman who gave no explanation of the meaning of the odd apartment. The woman whose shadow — crossing the shade that shrouded the room's only window — revealed nothing. One might only speculate about her frequent visits to this supposed place of worship – or memory.

Laughed Over Love Letters

But everything was not solemn at Winchester place.

Once upon a time, the June moon hung low over the great palms and cypresses. Its light shone silvery through the wall of feathery bamboo, as the scent of many flowers pressed against the face of the great house. It was a pressure like something tangible.

It was then that Mrs. Winchester laughed heartily when she told of letters she had recently received.

Love letters! Ardent letters. Two of them from a young man in San Jose.

He was vehement in his protestations of undying affection. He wrote, with flourish and pronounced literary flavor that he loved this woman who was many years his senior.

No mention of her wealth – horrors, no! Just love – his young love for a rich elderly widow, written violently in bright sunlight; but told and laughed over by the one ardently addressed – laughed over when the June moon shone on young lovers.

And, speaking of Mrs. Winchester and love – she once sent for a Gypsy palmist and have her fortune told.

Visit of Gypsy Palmist

The dark-skinned, gaily dressed,

midnight-eyed teller of fortunes arrived at Winchester Place. She was conducted to the little reception room at the head of the side staircase.

There awaited the lady of the manor – and her inevitable secretary.

As is usual, the Gypsy directed her palm be crossed with silver – designating two bits as the magic needed.

Mrs. Winchester is said to have done the usual thing. She directed her secretary to give the Gypsy two bits.

The fortune teller shook her dark head until the great gold loops of her earrings jingled.

"No good. No tell fortune for other woman's money. You give it to me – *your* two bits."

So Mrs. Winchester, who disliked obeying another's orders, put the bit of silver in the woman's hand.

The Gypsy's husky hand slipped the "two bits" into a capacious pocket. Then, the fortune flashed out in words as vivid as a film drama on the silver sheet.

"You will live to be very, very old," declared the Gypsy. Then, with a shrewd glance at the Queen Victoria-looking individual whose hand she held, the dispenser of fortunes continued:

"If you spend all the great money you have you will marry again."

And it was even as the fortune teller had said – old-age and no marriage. However, a suitor *had* come, bombarding Winchester Place and the heart of the wealthy widow with his ardent love appeals, appeals from May to December.

Young Lawyer Loses Chance

This story is from the great yellow house in the days of long ago — the days of the matched teams and the gold mounted harness and the proud Victoria.

It's from around the time when seven workers were hired to do nothing but trim the hedge – the hedge that, after Sarah's death, are straggling with uncut branches of cypress. Those same branches that now reach out into the light and up toward the sun. It's as if they're glad to escape the *snip-snip* of pruning shears in the obedient hands of seven Japanese gardeners.

But — according to the story from some years ago — a young attorney was given a small commission for Mrs. Winchester. The task was small. He needed only to look up one or two matters.

The young attorney saw it as something else. In fact, he held a rosy vision of being retained as the wealthy woman's advisor.

And then he lost his chance.

When he'd completed the small task for which he'd been hired, he needed to submit his bill. But how large fee to charge the wealthy widow? The work had been brief, but it involved some important matters.

A friend advised against the attorney asking more than two dollars for the work done.

Instead, the naive attorney saw a great opportunity. He mailed a bill for $40 – and never had another chance to retrieve his mistake. Too late, he realized his folly. When he described her, it was as many did, saying "her eyes could look right straight through you."

Charity Like Flowers

A strange life. A lonely life. But one that must've given some happiness, some secret satisfaction to her.

She chose her way of living and adhered to the original plan to the day of her death.

For more than 40 years, she is said never to have entered the church, never to have seen a movie, never to visited another's home.

And during these long years, she never rode in a railroad train.

But she built and built and built. And then tore down and tore out and built everything all over.

Over time, the original comfortable home became a great pile of lumber, famous for its apparently infamous architecture.

Despite that, some say that Mrs. Winchester was "a kind of an architect."

Who are we to criticize? Who are we to smile? Who are we to recount the strangeness of something none of us will ever understand?

Something in each life determines its trend.

Something not one of us can explain to another impels toward this or that determination.

Mrs. Winchester had her own philosophy of life and sufficient money to dare to be different.

While we may smile at the architectural "unrest" of Winchester Place, we will do well to remember her magnificent charities.

We should remember that, yes, she caused walls to be erected and then tore them down.

She also caused the gardens to be planted, the wonderful flowers to be propagated in the conservatories.

I believe that, in all the world, there was no cleaner, saner or more heartwarming worship of beauty than the love of flowers.

Let our memories of this neighbor – a woman who lived apart, for some good reason of her own – be as gentle as the blossoms with which the rare vases at Winchester Place were filled.

Let us think charitably of the woman who, not long ago, gave an order that the treads of a certain flight of stairs should be lowered and made easier for climbing. That was an order that holds pathos.

For, with all her great wealth, and with all her astonishing differences in living, Sarah Winchester came to the time when aged feet grew weary and climbed heavily toward the hope-starred night that men called death.

About the Winchester Mystery House

The Winchester Mystery House is a mansion in San Jose, California, that was once the personal residence of Sarah Winchester, the widow of firearm magnate William Wirt Winchester. It sits on about six acres in a lovely part of San Jose.

The house is located at 525 South Winchester Blvd, San Jose, CA.

Daily tours are available, as well as special events focusing on the many unique features of the property and its fondly remembered owner.

For more information about the Winchester Mystery House, visit their website: http://www.winchestermysteryhouse.com/

Made in the USA
Las Vegas, NV
08 December 2024

13513347R00046